HARVEY SMITH

BEDSIDE JUMPING

HARVEY SMITH

BEDSIDE JUMPING

Illustrations by Bill Tidy

Willow Books
Collins
Grafton Street, London
1985

Willow Books
William Collins & Co Ltd
London · Glasgow · Sydney · Auckland
Toronto · Johannesburg

British Library Cataloguing in Publication Data
Smith, Harvey
Bedside jumping
1. Show jumping
I. Title
798.2'5'0924   SF295.5

ISBN 0 00 218182 7
First published 1985

Made by Lennard Books
Mackerye End, Harpenden
Herts AL5 5DR

Editor Michael Leitch
Designed by David Pocknell's Company Ltd
Production Reynolds Clark Associates Ltd
Printed and bound in Great Britain by
Butler & Tanner Ltd, Frome, Somerset

Cover illustration by John Ireland

CONTENTS

DOGS AND PONIES FIRST

I used to play cricket at school and I was all right at it, but I was much more taken with animals. My brother had a horse which he rode round the moors at weekends, and he got me on a pony when I was seven or eight. The first time he put me on it, that pony frightened me to death.

My brother had some goats, and all of a sudden they came round the corner. The pony shot off, threw me on the floor and for six months I wouldn't get back on it. Early shocks and falls are all part of the game, but now I always say that you can't have a pony that's too old or too slow when you're teaching a beginner to ride. What they need most of all is time – time to build up their confidence and to learn what they're on about.

At least I wasn't run away with. That's the worst thing that can happen. Suddenly this animal underneath you is belting along at thirty miles an hour and it may take you anywhere. It may gallop into a car, into a stone wall – you may never live to know what it ran into. Much better to find a real old 'un that's good and slow and won't run anywhere. Once a horse has run away, it will run away again. They always do. People today go on about safety harnesses and safety hats – it's the horses they want to be spending more time on, not the outfits.

Well, I did get back on the pony and started going round on it with my brother. After a while I started going in for competitions in the local gymkhanas around where we lived in Gilstead, near Bingley, and from there I went on to jumping. In between, I had another period away from the pony when I was keener on dogs.

The Athelford Alsatians

My first dog was a little black and white working sheepdog. She came off a local farm and I swapped her with a feller called Tooey Blackpenny for a pair of bike handlebars. I was ten or eleven and I took her home in my zip-up jerkin. When I went indoors with this little puppy's head poking out of my jerkin, my mother went mad.

I called her Lassie, and I soon found out she was a freak dog. She was one of those intelligent creatures who only need to be shown something once and they never forget it. I could teach her a new trick in about five minutes.

If I wanted her to fetch an egg from the kitchen, I only had to

show her where it was, and then go back into the next room and say to her: 'Egg. Fetch it.' She'd go straight in there and carry it out. I had her jumping through hoops, then fire hoops, and soon enough we had a little circus act between us.

A pal of mine down the road saw this happening, and he started us performing in public. He used to train sheepdogs, and he had a daughter who played the saxophone. He was going to enter her for the talent competition at Bingley Gala in 1951.

'I'm going to enter you as well,' he said to me.

'Me?' I said, 'What for?'

'You and t'dog,' he said.

So I went down with Lassie to do an audition and we were in. On the night we finished up second. A girl singer won it. I was well pleased with how we'd done, because that was my first appearance in public on a stage.

Afterwards, I was approached by a feller from Bingley who had a troupe of dogs called the Athelford Alsatians. He wanted me to go with him, and I did. At weekends and in the school holidays I went all over the place with the Athelford Alsatians – to fairs and fetes and country shows. I did five to eight minutes with Lassie, showing off all her latest tricks, and by then she had quite a repertoire.

She could fetch a beer bottle for me, then go and get me a glass. I had her pick up an egg and carry it over to a four-foot stand, jump the stand with the egg in her mouth, then bring it to me and I'd crack it into a glass. I had her jump on my back and ride me. She was a brilliant dog. While I was with the Athelford Alsatians I bought an alsatian as well, but that dog was a complete dumbo compared with the little black and white sheepdog.

I was a bit wild in those days, with no great liking for school. Having the dogs made it easier for me to dodge off. I let them follow me to school, then a few minutes later I'd say to the teacher: 'Oh look, my dogs are outside.' So then I had to take them home, and that was me off school for the rest of the day.

There were other times when I fell out with the authorities. I got a severe caning one day from the headmaster. I thought it was too hard so I kicked him and called him a 'graded old bugger', and ran off. They found me two days later in Baildon at Amby Ainsworth's place. He was a gypsy, a local character, and I knew I could stay with him if I needed to keep out of the way.

Amby was a law unto himself, the kind of feller who appealed to kids like me. I'm not sure if he had magic powers, but he impressed

9

me one day when a mouse ran across the floor of his house. Amby reached out, no trouble at all, caught the mouse and bit its head off.

I'M EVEN BETTER WITH WHIPPETS. OPEN THEM TRAPS...

Middle Farm

Back with horses, my brother and I started working with the pony in our spare time at Middle Farm, which is just down the hill from where I live now. My brother got the bits together to make a cart and we turned ourselves into a delivery service.

In the holidays, I walked up five miles from our house in the village, took out the pony and cart and delivered milk all the way down the hill, through the village and into Bingley. In the town, there were two mills which belonged to a firm called Beavers. After I'd moved the empty milk crates out of the way, I used to carry wool from one mill to another – top Beavers to bottom Beavers – shifting maybe twenty bales in a day. Then I'd drive back up to the farm, see to the pony and go home.

My brother and I were often up at the farm until late at night. Before we left, the farmer's wife always made us a cup of tea, then she gave us a bun each for the journey home, which we did either on foot or two on a bike – we only had the one bike between us.

The tea was alright but we stopped eating the buns when we found out where she was getting them from. This farm also did a pig round, collecting up pig swill from round about, and one of the places

10

they called at was a bakery. When the cart got back to the farm, she used to pick out all the buns that looked a bit reasonable and hand a couple of them to me and my brother. We still took them off her, even when we knew, then on the way home we threw them out to the sheep on the moor.

11

Middle Farm worked completely on horsepower. They never even had a tractor until nine years ago, and in the house they made no allowances for personal comfort. Everyone who lived there survived to a ripe old age – the last feller there was 94 when he died – but I'm not sure how they did it. There was no electricity. They had one coal fire with a Yorkist range which they used to heat the water and cook the joint. The rest of the cooking was done on a Calor gas ring. In the living room they walked on an old flag floor – no carpets anywhere – and the only light was from a Calor gas lamp. All over the rest of the house they used paraffin lamps, and even down in the stables and cowsheds, where they used to milk at night, it was paraffin lamps too. They did the washing in an old stone sink, one side of which was all worn down at the top from sharpening knives. There was no inside toilet – just a seat and a bucket in an outside shed. They had a bath in the bedroom, and that room was separated from downstairs by floorboards only. They had no ceilings as such; in theory the heat from downstairs rose up through the cracks in the boards and heated the bedroom above. In the bedroom itself there was no ceiling either; if you looked up, you were looking at the slates – and sometimes the stars.

That farm was a real taste of old Yorkshire. You can almost imagine them standing round the old coal fire inventing a few of those rhymes for which Yorkshire people are famous. Rhymes like this:

'Lending, spending and giving away
Is a thing you can do any day.
Begging and borrowing
And making your own
Is the hardest thing you've ever known.'

First Jumps

That kind of talk may sound a bit over the top these days – especially to Southerners! – but when I was learning to jump horses it was all make do and mend. My jodhpurs never saw the inside of a shop – my mother made them, and the pony that jumped our home-made fences and farm walls was the self-same one that worked the milk round.

My father had a building firm – he built a lot of the houses in our village – and after I'd been going well at the local horse shows, he let my brother convert the wagon he used for work into a pony transporter. To do this, he got an old house door, and fixed it with hinges at the back of the wagon to make a ramp. The pony jumped up the door into the wagon which had a sheet of canvas over the top, and off we went to a show.

Jumping in those days was much more low-key than it is now. There was no dressing up – if you had boots, breeches, a jacket and a flat cap, you were ready to go. It wasn't that long since the war, when

13

there'd been nothing going on at all, and in the early Fifties a new generation of young lads was coming through at these little local gymkhanas. It was all very informal and I used to go in for everything with that pony – the apple and bucket race, musical chairs, bending poles – it was a different world back then, so much so that today's young kids wouldn't know how to do it.

In fact, when we have special events now, like a two-horse race or a bareback competition, the younger showjumpers can't get near me – even at my age – because they never learnt it when they were starting out. (A two-horse race, by the way, is where you jump the fences one way, then switch to a second horse and gallop back the way you've come – and the trick is to fly across from one horse to the other in next to no time.)

At Middle Farm we either jumped the farm walls or used a couple of fences we made ourselves. We had a bush fence and a door which we made into a wall with two bits of wood knocked into the side which had nails sticking out at various heights so we could keep pushing the pole higher and higher.

The next step was to keep horses down near home in Gilstead. Our training ground was at a quarry which my father had. On one side of the quarry was little three-acre paddock – with a sixty-foot drop on the far side – and we jumped the horses up there. We raced and jumped those horses like you wouldn't believe, and never gave the drop a second thought.

I was still at school when I got my first good horse, Farmer's Boy. I wagged it away from school one day with a pal of mine and we went to York Horse Sales. We saw this big raw-boned horse which I just knew I wanted. I didn't know a thing about how to judge a good horse, he probably winked at me as he went past and that did it.

He fetched 33 guineas in the ring and when I went and saw the feller who'd bought it he said he'd sell it on to me for £40, to include his commission. So I rang my Dad at home and asked him if I could have it.

He said: 'I thought you were at school.'

'No,' I said, 'I'm at York Horse Sales.'

He thought about that for a bit, then he said: 'Go on, then. You can have it.'

I put the horse on the train at York, and he came into Bingley Station that evening. He was an unbroken horse, and I took him down to our stables at Gilstead, which was another of our home-made jobs knocked up from a load of corrugated tin sheets. That night the horse

14

jumped straight out the window and took the window frame with him. Next day I went to work on him and within six weeks I had him in his first show.

Farmer's Boy was a natural genius, like the dog. It may have been fate, but I knew I was lucky to have been in the right place and found him when I did, just as I was lucky to be presented with the dog. Those two animals were so good, they gave me the best beginning I could have asked for.

THE SHOW HITS THE ROAD

When I brought Farmer's Boy to Bingley by train, an era was coming to an end. Just earlier, when people like Ted Williams were travelling round the agricultural shows, they went all over England by railway. It was a completely different routine from what we have today with our road wagons.

If they had a show, they set off from home first thing in the morning and rode maybe five or ten miles to the railway station. The railways had special freight wagons with horse-boxes inside, so the horse went in one of these and the rider went in an ordinary passenger carriage. They travelled maybe fifty or sixty miles, then got out at the nearest station to the show, rode another five or ten miles, did the day's jumping, rode back to the station, had a fifty or sixty-mile train ride, then rode five or ten miles home – and that was a day's work. Can you imagine people doing that today?

If they had a two-day event, they shacked down anywhere, often beside the horse. In the morning they went round to the stockman's tent to get a bit of breakfast, then round to the cattleman for some milk, and that's how they went on.

When you compare the railway style of travelling with the wagons we have today, you can hardly believe it's the same sport just a few years later. Today a good wagon carries six horses, and up front there is plenty of sleeping room, a shower and fitted kitchen, and the whole thing is wired for electricity that we hook up to as soon as we reach the showground.

Thirty years ago, I can remember it being rough when we had our first wagons. I went down to London for the first time in 1954 in an old Dodge, which my Dad bought for me for about £300. He died in 1956 and all the wagons in his firm were sold, which left me with only the horses. I went and bought an old furniture van for £35, a petrol-driven Albion. We put a new door on the back of it and away we went. I had my bed above the cab, and there was room for two horses. Each time we started the engine, we had to give it half a swing on the handle – it went every time.

The next wagon was also an Albion, and had been used for carrying ovens. My brother and I dismantled it, put in a Ford 4D engine and turned it into a flying machine. It flew for us until the day we were coming back in a hurry from the Royal Highland Show in Edinburgh. A wheel came off when we were doing sixty miles an hour and the wagon tipped over with three horses and my farm man, Willie Halliday, in the back.

Willie had been making a brew of tea. I climbed out and walked round the back. Everything was upside down and I had to open the door sideways. Willie was all right and we pulled the horses out, then a stove and pots and pans and what was left of the boiling water. There was steam everywhere. Farmer's Boy was one of the horses, and all three were unharmed, except for one which had a scratch about three inches long on its neck. We put them in a field next to the road and thought about what to do next.

Then along came a feller called David Barker (who went to the Olympics in 1960). He pulled up when he saw our wagon and asked us what had happened.

'We had a bit of a calamity,' I said. 'We've put the horses in that field over there.'

'Aye,' he said, looking round, 'but where's your dog?'

'Oh!' I said, 'I forgot t'bloody dog.'

We went round to the front of the wagon and found the dog still in there, sitting on the dashboard, right as rain. Luckily David had room in his wagon for six horses, so we put our three in with his three and he dropped us home in Bingley at five o'clock in the morning. At ten o'clock we went to a show at Skipton with the same horses – and won the class.

Curse of the Caravans

The worst period in the history of our travels was when we all thought the answer to our problems was to tow a caravan behind the wagon. Those caravans were a disaster. They did nothing except give trouble, flying off into hedges and into buses, you never saw such a mess. Two or three riders were so fed up they abandoned their caravans on the motorway – took the plates off and pushed them over the bank.

I know how they felt. The most awful thing you can tow is a caravan behind a wagon. We came to dread those night journeys, trying to get home at two or three o'clock in the morning when the damned caravan was swinging about behind, then sparks flew on the road as the towbar broke and suddenly the caravan was past you and heading for an almighty collision if there was something else on the road.

We were on our way to Edinburgh with a brand-new caravan. Willie was watching it out of the window. It was a handsome-looking caravan and we were very proud of it.

'Is it there, Willie?' I called out.

'Yes, it's on, I can see it . . . It's off!' he shouted.

As we drew away from it, the bloody thing skewed off the road and ploughed into a fence. Caravans. They were a nightmare interlude in our lives and we all praised the Lord the day we got our first all-in-one wagon, built on a coach chassis with horse-box and caravan combined. At last the rough times were over (though we still keep our fingers crossed).

THE LAY OF THE YORKSHIRE TRAVELLER

She was Nancy when in Bognor,
She was Susan when in Perth,
She was Nellie when in Blackpool,
The sweetest girl on earth.

She was Mavis when in Brighton,
The finest of his bunch,
But down on his expenses
She was petrol, oil and lunch.

AFTER FOXHUNTER

When I first started in showjumping, the legend was Foxhunter. I now do a song about the sport, which says what gipsies we all are, and the opening lines go like this:

'They say Foxhunter's name
Brought showjumping to fame
When Sir Harry cleared five foot two . . .'

To me, Foxhunter laid the foundations for everything the sport has today – an international following, big television audience, sponsorship, and all the works.

Foxhunter became a hero in the 1952 Olympics, when he was the only British gold medal. His success captured the heart of the country just as showjumping was beginning to be seen on television – and just as television itself was getting off the ground.

It wasn't a fluke in any way that Foxhunter had that victory, because he was a very good horse. He won something like seventy-four classes for his country. He wasn't that old when he finished, about twelve or fourteen. He flew the flag for Britain all round the world, jumped in Nations Cup matches, Grands Prix – he did a great job to put showjumping on the map.

Without him, the sport wouldn't be where it is today, so much so that when I started in it they'd just launched a 'Foxhunter' competition, sponsored in those days by the *Daily Express*. It was seen as a way of gathering all the young talent together from all over the country, and staging a big final at Harringay. That later shifted to Wembley, but the important thing is that the competition is still running, and to me it counts as the biggest competition in the world to be run every year. Each and every horse in England has a chance to prove himself and go to Wembley – and come out the No 1 horse. It's a super idea, and it's rightly dedicated to the horse that got showjumping off the ground.

Sir Harry Llewellyn is still a great follower of the sport. He pops up all over the world and you don't know where you're going to see him next. This year he popped up in Dortmund. He enjoys life to the full – he hasn't stopped enjoying life since he won the gold medal in '52. He goes photographing animals in Africa, then in Germany he was photographing birds. Wherever he is, he is always switched onto showjumping – where it should be going and what it should be doing.

He can buy and sell a lot of the younger ones who are trying to run it today. He's an old man now, but you still won't get much past Sir Harry.

Pegasus

This was another great horse of the same era as Foxhunter. He was no more than a pony, about 15.1, just a little grey horse. But the way he went round a ring was unique. He would run down and give every fence six inches to spare. He was so light on his feet, if you closed your eyes at Wembley or one of the indoor shows, you never heard him take off or land.

If Pegasus was around today, he would still be winning as many big classes as he did in his own days. For five or six years on the trot he won the leading money in England. They took him to the States in about 1958, and today Ted Williams is still the only man to win the four American Grands Prix – he won in Harrisburg, in Washington DC, New York and Toronto.

That is the mark of the horse's stature as a competitor. And yet, to look at him, he was a little thick fat cob, no more than a pony, more fit to pull a cart than go showjumping. To the world he may have been Pegasus, but at home they called him Porky.

Flanagan

Flanagan was a really nice type of horse. He was bought in 1954 by Robert Hanson for his son, James, who jumped a lot but tragically died of cancer the same year. Old Bob Hanson, a Yorkshireman from Huddersfield, was a great supporter of showjumping and he kept the horse for quite a few years. Funnily enough, the first open competition I ever won, with Farmer's Boy, was at Barnsley Show, and I shared first place with Flanagan who was ridden by a feller called Jim Cowan.

Shortly after that, Pat Smythe took the horse over. At first I'd thought he was only going to be a speed horse, because he was very fast against the clock, but then Pat started putting him in bigger competitions, in Nations Cups and the like, and he really developed into a good horse. Not the best, or the most versatile – he would have been lost in the Olympic Games or the World Championships – but round the international circuit he was very useful.

Flanagan saw Pat through to the end of her showjumping days. He was an honest, bold horse who always put his best foot forward. All you can ever ask of a horse is that he tries and keeps going, and Flanagan did all that and more. The only flaw in him I can remember is that he was a bit inclined to put a foot in the water. A lot of horses in their latter years start to go in the water. Apart from that, Flanagan was a good, big-hearted competitor.

O'Malley

Flanagan was one of a great trio of horses that Robert Hanson got together. The next one, O'Malley, he bought in Canada off Jimmy Elder. When he came over here, Dick Stilwell rode him for two or three months and then I was given him to ride at the Great Yorkshire Show. That was the same year I won the John Player Trophy with him, and he developed into a really good horse.

O'Malley went for three years as the leading moneywinner in England. Then Bob Hanson, being a staunch old stubborn Yorkshireman, decided he wanted to change the agreement I had with him. In those days we used to divide the horse's winnings three ways: a third for the owner, a third for training him and a third for the rider. So I had two-thirds, one of which covered all the expenses of keeping, feeding and looking after him all through the year.

After the third season, Old Bob wanted to see me. 'Well, lad,' he said, 'tha's been having too good a do with that horse.'

I said: 'How do you mean, Mr Hanson?'

He said: 'In future, you're going to have to give me half his winnings.'

Well, I had a little reckon-up, and there was no way I could give him half the winnings and make the job pay. I thought to myself: You can lay in bed for nowt as well as work for nowt. It's no good carting that horse around if it's just for a bit of honour and glory.

So I said to him: 'I'm very sorry, Mr Hanson, but you're going to have to take him back, and let somebody else have him. I can't keep him on for those terms.'

Well, he told me he had someone who would look after the horse for half his winnings. 'Good luck to him,' I said. Next morning, he called round early and by seven o'clock O'Malley was out of my yard.

That horse went for the next three years without winning a competition. To me that was moral justice. After three years I bought him back, but he wasn't the same horse as he had been when I let him go.

In his good years he was a very good puissance horse. He would run down to seven foot or more any day of the week. Today, horses are jumping seven foot six, but when O'Malley was in his prime there was never a horse to take him. Seven-two, seven-three – he'd outjump them so completely, he never had to go again, so he never got a chance to go for the big one. But I can say one thing: if he'd been given it to do, he'd have jumped higher than a cathedral. As long as you pointed him at something, he ran down and jumped it.

O'Malley won Grands Prix, puissances and big competitions all over the world. He's got to go down as one of the greats.

WAIT! THERE'S A HORSE ON THE ROOF...

24

Merely-a-Monarch

The third of Bob Hanson's trio was Merely-a-Monarch, which Anneli Drummond-Hay rode in her early days. This horse was bred out of a 13.2 pony by a horse called Happy Monarch, and he finished up 16.3 hands high – a very big animal but cheeky as well.

Ponies have that little bit of devilment in them, and that's what Merely-a-Monarch had. He had such jumping ability, he could go a foot wider than anything else and never get in trouble. In fact, before he came into showjumping, he was winning some really good three-day events.

He was such a good all-round horse, it seems strange that he was bred out of a 13.2 pony. When you go hunting, or to a cross-country event, you know you'll see a lot of big thoroughbred horses galloping on. But you'll also see a scraggy 13.2 pony with them, and ponies like that are every bit as good as horses to run and jump and gallop. The bit of pony breeding in Merely-a-Monarch made him that little bit freakish – as he was.

Mr Softee

Another horse out of Yorkshire, Mr Softee was owned by the Massarella family. I think Old Andrew bought him to start with and passed him on to John. I first saw him at Falkirk in 1958, jumping in a novice competition and I thought: What a good horse.

In those days he was known as Foxhound. As he improved, he started going in the big county shows, but we never saw the best of him until David Broome rode him. David and this horse got a partnership together that was exceptional. He was a very careful horse and wouldn't take fences down. He would always go in and give his best and he was very fast against the clock.

He had a marked physical peculiarity: he was really bow-legged behind. Like one of those old footballers. He looked like his name, Mr Softee, with his four white legs and all bowed at the back. You might have thought, to look at him, that he wouldn't have stood up to showjumping, but once he got going with David he went all the way to the Olympic Games. He didn't have the greatest ability, but he and David believed in themselves and in Mexico they came out third in the individual competition. He also won the European championship and he was unlucky not to win the Hickstead Derby. He never had a fence down, but he slipped doing a turn on the flat, which cost him eight faults.

Mr Softee was a high-class all-rounder, good in the Nations Cup, and good for his country.

Stroller – and Dundrum

Stroller was incredible, there's no other word for it. Even so, let's also remember Dundrum, because a lot of people think of the two together. Dundrum and Stroller. They were both by the same sire, a horse called Little Heaven.

Stroller jumped in a lot of pony classes, winning regularly at 14.2. Then – and this is what's amazing about him – he came out of pony classes and started carrying an adult around at the Olympic Games, World Championships, Nations Cups … One night in Antwerp I saw him run down and jump six foot ten. But when you're stood at the side of him, he's still a 14.2 pony and you can't believe he's just cleared this massive obstacle.

When he won the World Championship at Hickstead, David Broome and myself walked the course and we did not see how he could jump it. He did better than that. He beat a whole string of class horses like Flanagan and Merely-a-Monarch. He must have had a heart as big as a bucket. He kept jumping till he was a big age; he was nineteen or twenty when he finished and he was still jumping the big fences.

Dundrum was also reckoned to be small. He was 15.1, about three inches bigger than Stroller, and the way he jumped was unique. Where Stroller used most of his body to jump, Dundrum cleared obstacles like a deer. If he ran down to a big wall, seven foot two high, he would stand away between twelve and fifteen feet, which is a long way, in fact a normal horse wouldn't even get to the wall from there. Then he'd pick up and fly like a deer, and land as far away on the other side. A super horse.

Vibart

To go from Stroller and Dundrum to Vibart is about the biggest switch you could make. They couldn't have been more different. Vibart was out of a shire mare and he was built like a great big carthorse. His feet were like two dustbin lids, you've never seen a horse with bigger feet in your life. It was a treat to see Andrew Fielder wind him up – his tail would start going and his feet used to bounce in the air, and then he'd be away.

Vibart wasn't a prolific winner. He didn't win a lot of classes, compared with some others. He jumped a lot of clear rounds, and then got beaten on the clock. But he used to win the right classes, the big ones – the Hamburg Derby, the Aachen Grand Prix, the Leading Showjumper of the Year. That's just three for starters. Not many horses are good enough to win that kind of competition, but he was.

If you saw him, by the way, he had the ugliest big head on him, but he always had that famous kickback. He became a television star, just as Nice Feller did before him in the days of Foxhunter, when he was the big horse with the kickback who always did something.

People love horses which have this strong identity. As soon as it comes into the ring, they recognize its style and they know that something special is coming. To me, this is a little bit where showjumping has gone wrong today. The sport has got so far advanced that all the horses are being trained to jump in a similar style. They have to jump a bit bigger than they did in days gone by, and you can understand how the various styles have come closer together. But, for the sake of the sport, they've got to find a way for horses to establish a stronger identity with the public.

It's sad to say that showjumping has been losing ground in this respect. When Vibart was going strong, he and Andrew Fielder became legends. But, it's funny, when Vibart went, so did Andrew Fielder. You could see him around a few county shows, but he never again found a horse that could give him that same get-together as he had with Vibart.

With horses, it's like a marriage. If it's going to work, you've got to know the horse and the horse has got to know you. Then you can develop a special feeling between you. Maybe. Some horses suit you and some don't.

Harvester

Harvester was one of mine. He belonged to Bert Clements of York – a good old-fashioned horse dealer. He'd had Harvester as a young horse, broken him in, taken him round the local shows and started him jumping. Then for twelve months Bert pestered me:

'Take him,' he kept saying. 'He's better than you think.'

'No,' I always said, because I didn't think he was special.

'Have a sit on him,' said Bert to me one day at the Yorkshire Show. So I sat on him, then we jumped some fences and I finished up jumping some planks about five foot six high. Well, for a green horse that was good. So I took him.

The thing that made Harvester was, he'd done no work from when he was four years old until he was ten. Bert had taken him round a few shows and entered him in some little jumping classes, then taken him home and mothered him again. So he'd got to ten years old with no miles on the clock.

Within six weeks of his coming to me, he was starting to win big classes. And when he came out the following year, he was the leading moneywinner. After that he didn't look back for five or six seasons, and he became a very good, reliable horse. I would pick him as the most genuine horse I've ever ridden. If you turned a corner, and he had ninety per cent chance of missing a fence and only ten per cent chance of jumping it, he'd take the ten per cent and jump it.

His heart was so big and so golden, there was never any way he would go down without a fight. When you said to him: 'Come on, old lad, we're off against the clock now,' he was away. You could put him against the best, no matter who, and he'd win it for you.

He had such quality, he could go in and win a speed

competition *and* he could win a good jump-off competition. He also won quite a lot of Grands Prix. In those days, when I didn't know any better, I used to put him in puissances as well. He never did much, and a feller came up to me one day.

'Why ever do you keep putting that horse in puissances?' he asked me.

'To try and win 'em,' I said.

'It'll never jump more than six foot two as long as it lives,' he told me.

Well, it went on like that for three years. One night we were at the White City and I was in line to become Leading Rider. The puissance came along and I thought: Sod it. We're going in today.

That night Harvester came in and he jumped seven foot two. And he jumped seven foot two in every puissance he went in afterwards. It just shows that if they're game enough, they'll learn. He learnt how to jump the big wall. It took him a bit of time, and it wasn't natural to him, but once he'd learnt how to do it he never forgot.

Pennwood Forge Mill

This horse was bred in Ireland and he was a little bit strong for a showjumper. He was a good, bold horse, and it was a feller called Johnny Rothall who brought him out. He jumped him for a while around shows in the Midlands, and then Paddy McMahon got him.

Once Paddy and this horse were together, they struck up a great partnership. Everywhere they went they were winning, winning, winning. For six or seven seasons Pennwood Forge Mill jumped out of his skin for Paddy. He won him the European Championship, the Leading Jumper, the King George V Cup and most of the best classes at Wembley.

The public took him over. It was a rags-to-riches tale, because he was bought very cheap, for about £1,900, and this combined with his winning ways to make him a legend. To the people who watched him and cheered him, he was like the horse-next-door, the one they could afford themselves, and so they felt that much closer to him.

For Paddy McMahon, he has been irreplaceable. Since he stopped riding him, he has tried a lot of other horses but he has never found a partner to compare with Pennwood Forge Mill.

Uncle Max

Uncle Max set out as an American rodeo horse and was buck-jumping for four or five years. Then a boy called Neal Shapiro got him and turned him into a showjumper, to such good effect that he was leading moneywinner in the United States for several years.

Neal Shapiro had ambitions to get on the US equestrian team, but the team trainer, a feller called Bert Nemethy, wouldn't have this rodeo horse because it used to fly-buck and do all sorts of silly things. So Shapiro sold the horse and he came to England, and Ted Edgar got him.

They were ideal for each other. All his life Ted was the clown of the showjumping scene, a man you could guarantee to go in and do something spectacular. Either he won, or the horse threw him over the fence or he finished up throwing the bridle at it. Ted was really good for the sport, especially for its following on television, and when he began riding Uncle Max everyone was very happy because they knew that sparks were sure to fly.

While Ted perfected the art of throwing himself out of the saddle and kicking his heels above his head, Uncle Max showed his own talents as a clown and they became firm favourites with the crowd. They were winners too. Both of them wanted to win every time they went out, and even if their plans didn't always succeed, they did win the King George V and a lot of big classes together.

When things went wrong for them, they went diabolically wrong. I remember Ted jumping in the Nations Cup in Aachen. He went down to a combination which, if it had stayed there from then until now, he would never have cleared. He went down to this combination four or five times in two rounds, and every time he finished up on the floor. But Ted and Uncle Max were always game. They never stopped coming back for more.

Boomerang

If you think of what happened to him later, this horse had a funny beginnning. The Edgars brought him over from Ireland, where they'd bought him off one Eddie Macken. Liz Edgar rode him, and he did well.

However, all his life he'd been a bit shuffly in front and the Edgars doubted if he'd stay sound, so when they were offered a lot of

money for him they said yes, and off he went to Holland for a couple of years. Only after that did Eddie Macken get him back, but as soon as he did, that horse started to win.

And when I say win! That horse could name his class. He seemed to win everything he went in for, which was bad for Eddie's ego because he got so big-headed you couldn't believe it! Showjumping is usually a very good sport for dealing with someone who has ego problems, but unfortunately it took about five years for Eddie's ego trip to run out. He won four Hickstead Derbies on the trot, two or three Hamburg Derbies, and nearly every Grand Prix he went in. All you ever saw in that time was Eddie Macken and Boomerang winning. All the other riders, including myself, were sick to death of Eddie Macken and bloody Boomerang. Whether it was on time, height or width, there was no class they couldn't go in for and win. The rest of us were left going for second place.

Then Boomerang was retired in 1980, and ever since poor old Eddie has been struggling to try and get a team of horses together. It's hard work, and recently a lot of people have been asking me why Eddie isn't going so well.

I tell them: 'His Boomerang won't come back.'

Anglezarke

This is a good horse. I remember being aware of him right from the word go, when my missus was travelling round the pony shows with the lads. She'd been into Lancashire one day, and when she got home she was telling me how our ponies had gone, and then she remembered something else.

'By the way,' she said, 'I've seen a very very good horse today. A lad called Adrian Marsh rode it. It's called Angle Iron or something like that.'

Anglezarke is a very genuine horse, and did well as a four and five year-old. He was bought very cheaply for something like £300, and the Maguire stable had him. To look at, he's a bit like Mr Softee – rather bowlegged behind, and has the same sort of swank and swagger about him. But he's an out-and-out jumper.

Adrian Marsh had two seasons with him. Then he got sold at Wembley for a lot of money to a secret buyer. There was a lot of speculation about who the new owner was, and names mentioned included Sir Hugh Fraser and Trevor Banks, but that was the talk in the paddock; no-one really knew who the actual owner was. Anyway, the Banks stable looked after him and travelled him, and he was ridden by Mick Saywell for a couple of years.

They used Anglezarke mainly as a speed horse, but really he wasn't all that good. He used to win the odd speed class, then kick a few down, and I was talking to Malcolm Pyrah about him one day when Malcolm was about to go with Mr Hunnable to buy a very good grey horse called Chainbridge from Trevor Banks.

'Don't leave the chestnut behind,' I said to Malcolm, 'he's a good horse.'

Just then Malcolm wasn't keen, but a couple of months later he had him for a week or two to try. He was man enough to come to me later and say: 'You were right about that chestnut horse. He is the better of the two.'

Since that time he's proved it. There's no track too wide, no fence too high for Anglezarke, and he's very fast against the clock. He's one of those freak horses which others can compete against and do their very best, but still not be good enough.

Anglezarke hasn't yet had the lucky break he needs to win a big one, but he's been very near a lot of times. He has been second in the European, second in the World Cup, second in the World Championships. Quite often a horse wins a championship and you never hear from it again. But Anglezarke has been so close on so many occasions, he certainly deserves to win a big one before he retires.

Ryan's Son

Another great horse – and a Yorkshire horse – is Ryan's Son. He's got to be a great horse if only for the number of fences he's jumped. He started jumping when he was four years old, and he's now seventeen and still in the top flight of showjumping.

When you look at him, he's just a little carthorse. Nothing else. I all but had him bought one day, when I was in partnership with Trevor Banks.

I said to him: 'Trevor, I'm going to have that horse.'

'How much is he?' Trevor wanted to know.

'Two thousand pounds.'

'Two thousand pounds for him?' yelled Trevor. 'I couldn't bear to look at his bloody ugly head over the door every morning.'

So we left him, and he went to John Whitaker. I tell you, that's the best day's work John Whitaker ever did. If he's been in thirty Nations Cups, he's ridden Ryan's Son in twenty-nine of them. That horse is a real servant, a real goldie. He goes in to win every class. No horse has ever jumped more double clear rounds in Nations Cups, or more Grand Prix double clear rounds, but strangely enough he's won very few Grands Prix. On the other hand, he's been second, third or fourth far more than any other horse.

He's had a couple of wins late on in his career, but he has suffered from being in such demand. In Nations Cups he always had to come out the day before and jump two rounds. He'd lose his edge that day, then he'd jump two rounds the next day. Comes the final round, which he had to jump on time, he'd be just that little bit tired and off his best, and he'd get beaten in the Grand Prix by something which hadn't started in the Nations Cup.

Team Sanyo Horses

Getting round to my own Sanyo horses, I've had some good ones. The original Sanyo horse was Sanyo Sanmar, and we still have him at the farm; people have written songs about him and he is a famous old showjumper.

When I first had him, he was a nine or ten year-old jumping in the Foxhunter classes. I knew he was a good jumper but he was one of those who wouldn't do a day's work. Some days he wouldn't go out of the yard, another day he'd come out and walk up the lane and then wouldn't go back in the stable. His previous owners had had the same trouble. They'd tried to drive him, they'd tried everything, but there was no way he'd put in a day's work.

Willie Halliday took him to a few shows and he won a few classes with him, but he was still roguish and you never knew what he would do. I had the final shoot-out with him one day at Leicester Show.

I was jumping in a Grade B championship. Off we went on the round, cleared the water jump and then we came to a stile, two from home. He napped it, and threw me so I landed about a hundred yards

THIS THRASHING IS SPONSORED BY FOSDYKES QUIRTS AND ROPE ENDS LTD...

away with the bridle in my hand. I didn't know what had happened. The horse must have decided he'd had enough, because the next thing he did was walk over to the gate. I caught up with him there, and got the bridle on him again. Standing by the gate was Michael Freer, who'd been a horse lad all his life. Once I was on the horse again, Michael hit him with a rope end and he started to buck. So I got my stick out and started to hit him. When they saw this, the crowd started to cheer.

The more I hit the horse, the higher he bucked and the more the crowd cheered. It's the only time I've got away with giving a horse a good hiding in a ring. The horse must have known he couldn't win, because all of a sudden he settled down and then off he galloped. I turned him in and we finished the course. After that day, he never looked right or left again.

Sanyo Sanmar, or Olympic Star as he then was, became one of the best servants I've ever had. He was asked to jump World Championship stuff when he wasn't physically capable of doing it, but he always gave it a go. He'd run down to a fence, throw his heart over and follow it. He wasn't the best horse, but he always worked and tried his best.

Now he's turned out in the field, and he's more or less retired. But if Willie fancies going to a show, he'll catch him out of the field and put him in the wagon – and I'll guarantee that horse wins it. Then he goes back in the field again. He did three last year – three shows and three wins.

Sanyo Sanmar has been a real good horse. To have been such a villain in his earlier life, and then to have become such an honest servant – it goes to prove something I've noticed all the way through my career. I've always said that good horses are made by an accident, and that accident at Leicester Show, on that particular day, made that horse.

I had another one – Music Centre. I'd seen him in Germany and this horse was so careful I couldn't believe it. Anyway I got on it, rode it a bit and bought it. I got it back home and it wasn't much good for a couple of months. In the meantime I'd been finding out about the horse and its background, and it turned out that the life history of Music Centre was truly one for the scrapbook.

It was bred in Leicestershire; it was related to Specify, which won the Grand National; it was related to Jungle Bunny, which Lionel Dunning rode; it started life with Ted Williams, and even in those days it used to stop and put him on the floor. That's just for starters. Then it went abroad.

It was sold to Willi Melliger, in Switzerland, and he had it for a few shows; it did the same with him as it had done for Ted, so he sold it to Austria. In Austria, a feller called Boris Boor rode it. By this time the horse was known as Abor. It didn't change its habits, so from Austria it went to Germany, to Dieter Hoster. He won a few classes with it, then it started putting him on the floor as well, and that's where I came into the chain.

When I got him back to England I changed his name to Graffiti and he was quiet for two months – and then he started to go. I took him to Hickstead and he won a couple of classes, and I thought: You're not going to be too bad.

In the four or five-year period that I rode him, he won more classes – and faster – than any horse I'd ever ridden in my life. He was a hairsbreadth from being another Boomerang; if he'd had Boomerang's heart, he would have been as good. He always had it in his head that he wasn't going to knock any jumps down, so for me the job was to keep him going.

At his best he was a really consistent, fast horse. I took him to Rome and he won four classes straight off the reel. He would keep this going for a long run, coming out every day and winning, and then – for no reason at all – he'd come out one day and fire you through a fence. No warning – there you were, picking yourself up off the floor with the bridle in one hand and poles all round you, wondering why, because there'd been no reason for it. Next day he'd come out and win again. He was never easy to fathom.

Everybody said he was just a good speed horse. Then one year, 1977, he won seven Grands Prix, just like clockwork. I took him to Aachen once, and he went in five classes and won the lot, including the Grand Prix. I took him there the next year – he wouldn't jump a stick.

That was the funny mentality of the horse. At the root of it, he was never enthusiastic about his work, so you had to push him, push him all the time. But he was such a natural jumper, and so careful, you didn't mind the hard work as long as he kept winning. Then later, when he lost a bit of his sparkle, I let the lads have a go with him, but that didn't turn out very well. Neither of them liked him that much, and even if they could still win classes on him, it was a lot of hard work. By then we had better horses around us, and we reached a point where it wasn't worth persisting with him.

So we pulled the lever on him, and let someone else have a go. He's still jumping today or, as you might say, they're still trying to jump him. But, whatever I say about his contrary nature, no-one can take away the fact that on his day he was a very fast horse. He was one of the few that could actually beat Boomerang nine times out of ten against the clock. Not over the biggest courses, but over the middle-sized ones he was really good.

Then we've got the present-day crew. There's Sanyo Olympic Video, who is capable of anything. He was second in the Hickstead Derby and he won the Mill Street Derby (the Irish one), and he should go well.

There's Galaxy – a very good speed horse, though it's time he moved up a gear into the top bracket. He is a really high-class middle-event horse, he's careful and fast and he wins a lot of competitions.

Sometimes, the way we name our horses must be confusing to anyone who isn't in the know. A horse like Music Centre, with an

interesting past such as he's had, must have felt a bit confused himself as each new owner gave him a new name – and with us he went from his German name to Graffiti to Sanyo Music Centre. Just to add to it, on the farm we used to call him Music Box.

Sanmar wasn't quite so complicated. We called him Old Ollie because he was Olympic Star before he got his Sanyo name. Technology was Fernando, so that's what we call him. Olympic Video is Brigadier Who – except that the girls call him Harry! It's queer how this happens, but it does. We have a grey horse called Alabama – he's known as Jim, because when he was a novice he was called Prince Jim and that name has stuck with him all his life.

Deister

I would say that this is the best Grand Prix horse on the circuit at the present time. Just of late it looks to me as if he's had a little bit too much jumping. I beat him, for instance, on Sanyo Technology in a World Cup qualifier at Den Bosch. I shouldn't have beaten him, but I did. Probably he'd just lost a bit of sparkle after the long winter circuit – from October to the beginning of May, with only January and half February off, it's a long go and at that time of year it's hard to stay one hundred per cent fit.

Deister used to be ridden by Hartwig Steenken, the young boy who got killed. Then Paul Schockemöhle got him, and over a long period of time they've put together a vast number of victories. He's one of those horses who goes better outdoors than indoors, but his consistency has been amazing. This year, at the time of writing, Paul hasn't done too many World Cups with him, so I would imagine he plans to give it some wellie in the outdoor season.

As well as being consistent, Deister is a versatile horse. He can win a Hickstead Derby, and he can win most classes he goes in for. He always looks to be going slow, and Paul Schockemöhle rides him in a funny style. Instead of going forward with the horse when he jumps, he goes sideways. The horse screws the other way to rectify it, and to see them going round is like watching a boat on a windy night; they're swinging about all over the place.

But the main point is, it works. Somehow Paul has perfected a way of riding that horse for maximum consistency. Deister has jumped so many clear rounds, it's unbelievable. Not many riders would complain about that.

PECULIAR SEATS

Since timing came in, you don't get the variety of riding styles that you did in the old days. Riders now have to be so precise, they haven't time to throw themselves out of the saddle like some of the veterans used to do at every fence. We'll probably never see their like again, but it would be a great shame if they were ever forgotten.

John Massarella was unique. When he came to a jump, he used to throw himself three foot in the air above the horse, and his legs and stirrup irons finished completely the wrong way up, pointing skywards on top of the horse's back.

Alan Oliver was another prime example. Even in his heyday, when he had his best horses, he used to ride very short and throw himself in the air. The idea behind it was for the rider to take his weight off the horse while it was jumping.

So, as they came to a fence, and just as the horse was about to leave the ground, these jockeys of the old school flung themselves up off the horse's back – and the horse followed them. They travelled over the fence as two completely separate bodies, then on landing they came together with an almighty thud and went on to the next fence.

One of the reasons why people don't ride like that any more is that courses have become much more complicated. In the old days a course was seven fences round the outside of the ring and finish. Now there are doubles and trebles, with two or three strides between obstacles, and the modern rider hasn't got time to do all the up-in-the- air stuff. He has to be much more streamlined – and in the process he automatically eliminates these funny mannerisms.

THE WHOOPEE CUSHION SADDLE

What to my mind was good about the old way was that everyone worked out their own solutions. They might ride really short, like Alan Oliver, or very long, like Raimondo d'Inzeo, who always had his feet rammed right down in the stirrups. Or they could be unique, as Tommy Wade was. He rode with one leg short and one leg long.

The Australians had another answer. When they came to a jump, they didn't throw their legs up in the air, they threw them out sideways. Kevin Bacon was really hot at doing this. I always remember him on his little black horse, Chichester, leaping upwards from the saddle with his legs stuck out at near right-angles to the horse. John Fahey, on a horse called Bonvale, used to do the same; so did Jeff McVean, when he first came over. All the Australians rode in this same style. Now they've gone the other way, and they're tying their feet down to the girth so they can't shoot up in the air. Instead of flying free, they're actually strapped to the horse.

Basil (David Broome) used to throw his legs about a bit, but now he straps his feet into the stirrups. He puts rubber bands round his stirrup irons to hold his boots in place.

If there is one man who's been responsible for all these changes, it's Count Toptani. He wrote some very good books about riding some thirty or thirty-five years ago, and he invented the Toptani saddle which is still the model for most saddles designed today.

NO, HE READ
COUNT DRACULAS
RIDING BOOKS

Even though this has brought a lot more uniformity in the way people ride, you can still pick out some funny national styles. The Americans, for example, sit very upright, with the reins held high, as if they're knitting. The French like to lean forward when they go into a fence and row with their arms as if they're in a boat. The Italians lean forward as well, but they always ride very long, in the tradition of Raimondo d'Inzeo, whom we've met already.

Of course, there's no accounting for tastes, and I'm glad that some of today's riders insist on using this style or that style. Not many riders like taking jumps without their horse, but that's exactly what Basil did one day.

He went down a combination – three jumps in a row. The horse jumped the first, then as the horse jumped the second Basil flew off, landed backwards against the third fence and watched as the horse picked up and jumped the fence with him stood underneath looking up at it.

Not a lot of riders can do that.

THAT UNDERSEALING COULD DO WITH ANOTHER COAT

DAWN OVER HICKSTEAD

Dougie Bunn, the Master of Hickstead, travelled the world in the 1950s and came to the conclusion that in Britain we had no showground to compare with what they had abroad. He was good enough in those days to ride for British teams, so he reckoned he knew what he was talking about.

The old Hamburg Derby course, for example, had been going since 1920 and had an international reputation. Aachen was another – a huge arena with difficult natural obstacles. Bunny decided to make these his models, and he started planning his dream course that in 1960 opened at Hickstead in Sussex.

The impact on riders was immediate. Hickstead was harder and tougher than anything they'd seen before. When they went round to jump the massive natural obstacles for the first time, many of the horses were completely lost. Suddenly they came into a fence to find it had a big ditch underneath it. But Bunny wasn't satisfied with one ditch – he'd put in another one a stride after. The first time horses see them it's chaos – they're frightened to death.

THINK THEY'LL ALLOW DRESSING GOWNS

In my early days at Hickstead we thought that the best way to get on terms with these obstacles was to ride down to the ring very early in the morning and have a good look at what he'd built before the competition started. If we were early enough, and no-one else was about, we might even have a little spin round. When the class came up later in the day, the horse wouldn't be so frightened of the obstacles. It's not exaggerating to say that it takes two years to get a horse used to Hickstead – and in that time it can easily lose its peak form and then fade, so it's important to give a horse all the help you can.

Before we got this worked out, I landed up at Hickstead in 1970 with Mattie Brown. We'd come direct from Dublin and the horse was going really well. I was out exercising him at ten o'clock the first morning. There were a lot of people about, including some coursebuilders still working in the ring, and we went over to look. When I saw the double ditches I immediately thought: This little gangster's not going to jump those ditches.

I did no more at the time, but carried on exercising the horse and thinking about those obstacles. A few minutes later we were walking up at the top end, and I had a look round. There was nobody about, and before I knew what had happened, we'd jumped over the rail into the ring, jumped the double ditches and jumped out again.

I looked round, and not a soul had seen it. Not satisfied with what I'd done, I went and did it again. Into the ring, over the double ditches, and out again. Well, I thought, that was handy. When the time came for the Derby – a bit prematurely, as it happened – I was third to go on Mattie Brown and we had the only clear round.

This left a big piece of egg on the faces of the organizers, because hardly any spectators were there to see us. As there was such a large field for the Derby, someone had had the bright idea of running ten horses off before lunch and the rest afterwards. Each horse takes about four minutes to go round the course, so if you allow five minutes per horse you need something like three and a half hours to get through forty of them. That was why they decided to split the field, but when I went round on Mattie Brown there was hardly any public in. The people who paid to see the Derby turned up after lunch and found they'd missed the leading horse. No-one else could match us, and so that had to go down as a big boob on the part of the organizers.

The next year I went along to Hickstead but forgot to take the trophy with me, which didn't get things off to a good start with Dougie Bunn.

'Harvey,' he said to me, 'have you brought the trophy?'

'Oh, sorry Bunny,' I said, 'I forgot the damn thing. It's at home.'

He wasn't best pleased about that. 'Well,' he said, 'You'll have to get it back for Sunday.'

'Don't worry,' I told him, 'I'm going to win it again anyway.'

That really annoyed him. I wasn't his favourite rider that year in any case. Because of clashing dates I'd been at the Great Yorkshire and missed the first day of the Royal International at Hickstead, and then I'd been at Shrewsbury and missed the first day of the Derby. Bunny had retaliated by trying to have me thrown off the British team for the Nations Cup, but without success.

Next morning, I was up early with Mattie Brown and we had a good spin round to make sure the horse had remembered the ditches and dykes and all the rest of it. We finished and were just cooling off at the back of the grandstand, when I saw this grey horse come wandering down Bunny's drive.

It was a beautiful morning, but a bit early for most people – about half-past three or a quarter to four. I looked at this other horse and I thought: That's bloody queer, it's not making any noise. At that time of day you should be able to hear everything that moves, especially on Bunny's drive which is made of concrete.

I was intrigued by this silent horse, so I got a bit nearer to the ring. When it came to the end of the drive and went on the grass, they (who shall be nameless) stopped and removed a sack from each of the horse's feet. Then off they went for a gallop round the main ring, jumping a few fences while they were in there. I knew the horse, and it had a reputation for not liking the bank at Hickstead; next thing, his rider had taken him up there. They got to the end of the bank, and this horse definitely didn't like what it was being asked to do. So its rider hit it a couple of whacks with his stick and soon enough things were looking dangerous. The horse was turned to the bank and it was on the cards that it might go off it backwards.

The rider had enough sense to throw the towel in at that stage. He let the horse have its way for the time being and rode away – but then found that he couldn't get it off the bank at the other end. They were stuck.

From where I was watching I thought: I'll have a bit of fun here. I shouted out: 'Oi! What do you think you're doing?'

You never saw such instant panic in your life. The feller whirled round, alarm written all over his face, jumped off the horse, took the saddle and bridle off, and ran away leaving the horse on top of the bank.

Later that morning the Hickstead staff arrived and found, first of all, the horse still grazing on top of the bank – and then the rider came up to them complaining that someone had pinched his horse in the middle of the night!

At that time Bunny's show director was a feller called Major

Warren. He was a great old guy who used to get on well with everybody. One slight snag in his job was that Bunny used to make him sleep down by the ring in a caravan.

One day he said to me: 'Oh, Harvey, I'm bloody sick of this. I've had quite enough of it!'

'Oh, aye,' I said. 'What's going on, Bob?'

'That Bunny,' he said, 'he never stops nattering at me. He's even got me so upset, I dream about horses going past my caravan in the night.'

I said to him: 'Well, if it's any consolation to you, Bob – you weren't dreaming!'

That was how thing were in the early Seventies, since when old Bunny's grown a bit wiser. A few years later we tried to take another horse round the track for an early-morning spin, a very good horse which should have won the Derby except it was frightened to death of ditches. We got up good and early and off we went to give this horse a school. No luck. Bunny had been very crafty that time. Without saying a word to any of the riders, he'd had a car parked behind every fence!

Sammy's Signal

That year I forgot to bring the trophy back I had Bunny at me all week. 'Thinks he's going to win it again,' he kept saying. 'Pah!' He was delighted to tell reporters that I had no chance because he'd made everything a little bit higher and a little bit wider this year, so much so that my little horse couldn't jump them. Besides, he said, my horse was lame – which it wasn't.

So, came the day of the Derby, off I set on Mattie Brown. He was great. All he wanted to do was jump everything nice and clean and do his job properly. I thought to myself: By God, you're not going to have a fence down today. He was jumping really well. He came down off the bank with no problems, jumped the fence at the bottom of the bank and swung round, straight down to Devil's Dyke. When we jumped that, he just laid a toe on the rail. It bounced and bounced and bounced – and fell.

There's a spectators' box just nearby, on top of a hill, and Dougie Bunn and his cronies were in it. When he's up there, he doesn't think he's God but he does think he's His representative on earth. And when Mattie Brown had that rail down, they all cheered.

I thought: You bastards! And with that I grabbed hold of my horse, pulled him together and finished the track with four faults. Nobody else had a clear round, and we had to jump off against Buttermilk Boy. He went first and had three down, so that put us in with a great chance.

There was no way I was going to let my horse have another fence down, and he went round really well. When we got to Devil's Dyke again, he jumped that clean as a whistle and right there and then I could have eaten him, I was so pleased with the way he was going. Once I'd finished, I went round in a complete circuit and this brought me back to Bunny's little group in their box.

I saw them all up there with long faces and I thought: Serve you

right, you bastards. So then I swung the famous V-sign at them, bringing it up from somewhere near the horse's belly, like a boxer's uppercut. 'And up you too' was the message from me to them, and I felt a lot more relaxed when I'd delivered it.

The idea for this V-sign came from a Liverpool feller called Sammy Morphet, who I'd known for thirty years. We were at

Blackburn Show in 1956 for the first £500 class, with four riders in the jump-off. There was Seamus Hayes, Derek Kent, Alan Oliver and myself, and the prize money was £500, £100, and £50, and fourth place got a drover's breakfast – which is a pee and a good look round (or, nothing).

I was getting my horse, Farmer's Boy, ready for the jump-off when Sammy came rushing over. He stutters at the best of times, but just then he was excelling himself.

'Th-th-th-th-th-th-th . . .' said Sammy.

'Settle down, Sammy,' I said to him. 'What's up with you?'

'Th-th-th-th-they've cut up the bloody prize money and left you out.'

What he meant was, the other three riders had agreed in advance to share out the £650 between them, whatever the result. Riders sometimes did that, but what upset Sammy was that they hadn't bothered to consult me, assuming that I was definitely booked for the drover's breakfast.

'I'll tell you what, lad,' said Sammy to me. 'You get in that ring and – ! – give it to 'em proper.' In the middle of that last sentence Sammy blew a long mean raspberry, and combined it with a V-sign which started near the floor and finished above his head.

It was inspiring stuff. I jumped a clear round and pocketed £500, which left the other three with not a lot to grin about. In later years the memory of Sammy's V-sign stayed with me, and at Hickstead, when the sweet feeling of revenge was too much to keep to myself, I thought: Yes! And from Sammy and me, here's something for you lot up there – and gave it to 'em.

But I have to hand it to Dougie Bunn. We have our little ups and downs every so often, but there are never any grudges borne between us. At the same time he is the one man who has given British showjumping a course to match the best in the world. In fact, I would say that Hickstead is the hardest track in the world to jump. Everything that Hamburg had, or Aachen, Hickstead also has, but a little bit wider and a little bit higher.

If the ditches in Hamburg are four foot wide, Bunny's ditches are six foot wide. If the water there is fourteen foot wide, Bunny made his sixteen foot. Even his Devil's Dyke is modelled on one in Hamburg, called the Pulvermann, but the one at Hickstead is two foot deeper.

One result of this is that British riders have no fear of the courses they find on the Continent. The Hamburg Derby course is

53

now simple and straightforward compared with what it was before Hickstead was built. And, every year, Bunny sticks his neck out and makes his course that little bit more difficult to jump. As I may have said before, he's not an easy man but his heart's in the right place.

THE FATHER'S VERSION

When you've worked with horses most of your life, your kids don't stand much chance of getting into anything else. But you have to be careful, especially at first.

When we got married, we lived in a twenty-one-foot caravan. After eighteen months, our Robert came on the scene and it didn't take long, I'll tell you, to find out that living in a twenty-one-foot caravan with a squawking kid isn't much fun. Instead of just putting up with it, we decided we'd better do something.

Every night around seven o'clock, we used to get him bathed, changed and into his pram, then we wheeled him into the stable. That's where he spent his nights for the first two years of his life, so already there was a fair chance he'd turn out horsey. In the daytime we parked him next to the caravan, which was in a field, and horses used to come up and pull the blankets off his pram and bite his fingers and take terrible liberties with him. How he survived it all, I shall never know.

FOR GAWD'S SAKE, PLEASE TAKE HIM BACK IN THE CARAVAN

When Robert was eighteen months we bought a house in the village – at 19 Rylands Avenue – which was just across the way from the horses. We moved in there and then the other one arrived: Steven.

Up to when it was nine months old, it never batted an eyelid. It never moved, it never did nothing. All it did was have the dirtiest laugh; every time you pushed it in its belly, it used to laugh. Then at that stage, it thought it had better make a move, so it jumped up and started running. It ran everywhere; it wouldn't stop. Robert, aged two and a half, was still sat in his playpen, banging a wooden spoon on the floor, quite happy.

I said to the missus: 'Put that other bloody thing in the playpen with Robert.'

So, Horrible Horace went in the playpen. Within half an hour, the pair of them had climbed out of the playpen and they were off down the village to look for their grandma. Well, she lived two miles away, so they never had much chance of getting there. In the meantime, two kids that age, you can imagine them standing in the middle of the village, panicking.

The missus and I were all over the place looking for them, and when she came back with the pair of them in the pram I said to her, pointing at Steven:

'Listen. That thing there. It's got to be stopped. And I know how. If you've got a horse and it runs away, you tie it up. Same thing here. Get the harness out of his pram, put it on him, then get a clothes line and tie one end to him and the other to the drainpipe, and then you've got him. He can't run nowhere.'

One time we were up at the Royal Highland Show in Edinburgh. We had Robert with us; this was when he was still very young. It poured with rain for three days and it was really hot, muggy, clammy weather. We slept with the ramp down at the back of the wagon. At six o'clock in the morning we heard a knock on the door.

'Police,' said a voice.

We opened the door and this policeman had Robert with him.

I said to Robert: 'What are you doing out there?'

The policeman said: 'I found him wandering around the showground. He said he was fed up so he was off back to Bingley.'

Then Steven, when he was about three and a half, took it into his head that he wanted driving lessons. Our house was built on a bit of a hill, and in those days we had a Renault car. Steven got in, turned on the ignition and – chug, chug, chug – it was in reverse gear and off it went, straight through the garden gates and into the road.

As it went through the garden gates, Robert realized what was happening and ran after the car. He belted down the driveway, caught up with it, dived on to the bonnet and grabbed both windscreen wipers. Well, that's a bloody good way to stop a car going downhill, isn't it?

Luckily, one of the neighbours also saw the car going down the road, so he ran after it, pulled the steering wheel and turned the car into the front garden of a house a few doors down the street. It went straight into a greenhouse and smashed the lot up.

When I got down there, Robert was the first one I saw. I was just going to give him a belting when I thought: Nay, he was trying to stop it. Then the car door opened and this little face came out; ghostly white it was. I picked him up and I was going to give him such a crack…then I looked round and saw all the neighbours watching us out of their windows. So he got away with that one as well.

The only time I was allowed to babysit was one night when the missus was off to night school. She asked me if I'd look after the lads and I said: 'Sure. No problem.'

I'd checked to see what was on television and they had *Sportsview* and a couple of other programmes I didn't mind watching. The missus was no sooner out of the door when Robert – who'd been noisy when we were in the caravan – started up. I thought: I'm not going to have that bugger squawking all night, so I got hold of the treacle tin and took it up upstairs. I found a dummy, and gave it a good dip in the treacle and let him have it. I went downstairs and never heard another thing all night.

At about ten o'clock the missus came in. 'Have those lads been good?' she wanted to know.

'Marvellous,' I said. 'I never heard a word out of them.'

She went upstairs, and she hadn't reached the top step before she was turning round and yelling at me: 'Come up here!'

I went up, and looked. Yes, I could see what had happened all right. I'd left the treacle tin too near his cot, and he'd reached through and got it. He'd tipped it onto his head, his pillow was soaked in it, and there he was, really pleased with himself, sucking the biggest lolly in the world.

The other one – Steven – was all right, he was fast asleep. But it was my last go at babysitting. After that night, I was never allowed to do it again.

Jerusalem in Lancashire

Then I started thinking about getting ponies for them. The things I did and said that year were an object lesson in how not to do it. Talk about 'the proud father'! I'd bred these sons, and by the time they were five and six, I didn't mind who I told but they were going to be the best in the world. By the time they were six and seven, I'd frightened them to death.

All my friends around the shows could see what had happened. The boys wouldn't ride at all, in fact you only had to show them a pony and they'd throw a tantrum and scream.

I was over in Lancashire one day, looking at some horses, and I got talking to a dealer feller called Eli Warburton.

He said to me: 'Have you got your lads riding yet?'

I said: 'Between you and me, Eli, I've frightened them off it.'

'Oh,' he said, 'you did what I did, didn't you?'

'What's that?' I asked.

'Bought a flash pony, one that looked a million dollars. It ran away and scared 'em stiff.'

'You're right there,' I said. 'Bang on key.'

'Well,' he said, 'there's only one thing you can do now.'

I said: 'What's that, Eli?'

'Buy a donkey,' he said.

That's not a bad idea, I thought. Mind you, Eli had fifty to sell. So I took him up on it and we agreed a price.

'Right, Eli,' I said. 'Where is this donkey?'

'It's on your way home,' he said. 'Ten miles up the road. It's in a field. There's fifty donkeys in there and you can have your pick of them. There's just one thing. One of the donkeys is a big black 'un. Don't take that.'

59

'Why's that?' I asked him.

He said. 'It's my racing donkey.'

'All right,' I said. So me and Willie Halliday, my farm man, set off to look for this field. It was half-past ten at night when we got there and started going round all these donkeys. Well, I've never seen as many heaps of corruption in my life. Ears back, teeth gnashing at you, feet flying past your ear'oles – they were an evil bunch. All of a sudden, I bumped into one that didn't bite, kick or run away.

'Come here, Willie,' I shouted, 'I've got one.'

I never saw it close up in the dark, but we got it in the wagon and brought it home. At seven o'clock the next morning the phone rang. Eli.

'What's up now, Eli?' I asked him.

'You've got my racing donkey.'

It shows that if an animal does have good qualities, they'll come out. To have picked that one out of a crowd of fifty in a pitch-dark field, he must have had something. Spot on there, I thought.

So Eli let me keep him and I showed him to the lads. Straight off, they loved that old donkey. They called it Jerusalem and it was a real Christian. Let them do everything. The only thing it ever did wrong was one day it galloped under a tree with low branches and knocked the pair of them off. But that was the only thing. The rest of the time it let them maul it, pull it around, bash it – and it never ran away.

Anyway, that's how I got the lads started with riding. Then I had a pal over at Harewood called Jim Tempest. I went into his place one day and he was leading an old black and white Shetland pony out of a field. It was so lame, I'm not kidding you, it could hardly move. At that time of the year, in late spring, they get laminitis which is an inflammation of the foot brought on by the new grass. It seizes them up so they can't move.

I said: 'What are you doing with that old pony, Jim?'

He said: 'I'm going to go and have it knocked down.'

'Well,' I said, 'lend it to me for a month or two. I can use it to get my lads going.'

'I don't mind lending it,' he said, 'but it can't move. Your lads won't get much out of it.'

I said: 'It'll be fast enough for them.'

Anyway, I got it and took it home. In a month, you couldn't believe how well it had come on. I'd bought the lads a cowboy saddle when I was over in the States, and they had that pony galloping over the moors and round the land by the farm, playing at Tex Ritter and Cowboy Joe. They had a right do on this pony and he really got them going. He was old, and he wouldn't run away, but when he'd got sound he was just right for Robert and Steven.

First Jumps

So now we had Jerusalem and this Shetland pony. Then, while I was over in Dublin I bought a jumping pony called Drumcaid. It was just a bit big, nearly 13 hands, and got thrown out of the 12.2 class over there. I thought I could get it measured into 12.2 when I got it home – and I did. Mind you, I had a job pulling its feet down to make it look smaller, but we just got it in.

When I landed home with it I said to Robert: 'I've bought a pony.'

He said: 'What is it?'

'Well,' I said, 'it might jump a bit.'

I didn't tell him it could go over high walls and had been winning some good competitions in Ireland.

'Take it and ride it about,' I said.

So Robert got on Drumcaid and the little 'un rode the Shetland pony and they started running about the place and doing a bit of galloping. Robert was quite enjoying himself, and one day he said to me:

'Ey oop, shall we see if this pony can jump?'

So he was telling me that he wanted to try a bit of jumping.

'Aye, all right,' I said. 'Come on, we'll see what it can do.'

When you start jumping, you don't suddenly start trying to fly over fences, you start on the ground floor with one pole laid on the ground and you just get the horse to walk over it a few times. Then you trot over it, and then you gallop over it. After that you can try raising it in the air, but ever so gradually. Well, after a lot of playing about we'd got it up to all of eighteen inches, although at that height Robert looked more like he'd wobble off than stay on.

'Can we go to a show now?' he asked me.

'Nooooo!' I said. 'You have to jump three foot nine or four foot before you can go to a show.'

'Oh.'

'Listen,' I said, 'when you've jumped that high, you come and tell me.'

One day he came dashing in. 'Ey oop,' he said, 'I've just jumped three foot nine.'

He'd taken his mother's old tape measure out there to make sure he got it right. I checked the height and it was three foot nine. Then he came hurtling down again and jumped it.

'Can I go to a show?' he said.

I said: 'Nooooo! First you have to learn to jump eight or ten fences in a ring, and one of them'll be a double.'

Still, he was keen. So I set him up some fences. 'You keep jumping them,' I told him. 'You go round those twice or three times a week, or every night, and see how you go on.'

'Right,' he said.

One night I came into the house for my tea and sat down. I looked at the old lass. 'Where's that Robert?' I said.

'I don't know,' she said. 'He was in there watching television.'

I looked round. No sign of him. He wasn't upstairs. Half an hour later I looked out of the back window and saw that the lights were on in our riding school.

'Come on,' I said to the missus. 'Let's go and have a look.'

We went up the path to the school and I just parted the doors so there was a little nick we could look through. There was Robert on this pony, haring round the school at five hundred miles an hour. And he wasn't just content to be flying round the fences, he was doing Dorian Williams's commentary for him as well:

'. . . And Robert Smith goes into the lead. Thirty-two point six.'

'Raaayyy!' shouted Robert, on behalf of ten thousand spectators, and off he went again!

I opened the door and called him over. 'Robert!' When the pony came up to me it was all lathered up and panting like a dog.

I said: 'What are you doing with that pony?'

He said: 'I'm getting ready for a show. Can I go to one?'

This time I had a different answer for him. 'I think you can,' I said, 'and I think Dorian Williams is going to have to retire, an' all.'

'When can I go?' It was all he wanted to know.

I thought for a bit. 'Well,' I said, 'there's a show on Saturday at Honley, near Huddersfield.'

'Can I go?' he said, busting with excitement.

'Aye,' I said. I got him entered up, then I said to him: 'Whatever you do, get those girls of mine to tidy your pony up before you go.'

'Aye, all right,' he said.

On the Saturday morning I had some customers at the farm, so I was showing them some horses. I could see Robert messing about getting the pony ready. Then he led it down the passage and I saw it had one bandage on, one bandage off, not too clever.

'Oh, by the way, did you get one of the girls to straighten your pony up?' I asked him. 'Tidy its mane and tail?'

'Oh, no, no, no.'

'Well, you're not taking it to the show looking scruffy,' I told him.

'No, no, don't worry,' he said. 'I've done it myself.'

Well, if you've ever seen kids attack ponies with a pair of scissors, it's not a pretty sight. Its mane looked like the top of a castle wall, one step up, one step down, all the way along. It was living proof that you should never take scissors to a horse's mane or tail. That pony had lovely long hair which flowed out at the back of its legs. Or used to have, till our Robert went at it with his scissors. If it looked like anything, that pony was the little kid at school whose mother couldn't afford the barber. She used to put a basin on his head and snip up to it. What a mess – jagged bits everywhere. And when we got round to the tail, all that was left of it was a bristly stump. So that was his idea of getting the horse ready.

'Well, lad,' I said to him. 'You've made a good job of it. But, whatever you do, don't try it again.'

So he got ready to leave. All week long he'd been telling us, every time we sat down in the kitchen, how he was going to win at this show on Saturday, nobody else had any chance. He went on and on about it. Then, just before he finally left, the wagon was parked in the yard and he was leading his pony up to it – three bandages on, and one trailing on the floor – while our youngest was watching, tapping his fingers on the door post.

'Well,' he said, 'we'll see how Billy Boastful goes on today.'

I landed up at the show ground about four hours after they'd left home, too late to see him ride but I wanted to be there on the day. There was Robert, still riding his pony round. I couldn't understand it. One thing you can never get lads to do is to ride ponies for any time. They'll sit on for five or ten minutes, take all the glory, then they're off. But Robert was still riding. I thought: Bloody hell, he must have done well. So I got over to him and wound the car window down.

'Robert,' I called out, 'how did you get on in your first class today?'

He glared at me. 'How did I get on?' he said. 'I missed the bloody class.'

Marvellous. He'd had all that build-up, then he got to the show too late and missed the class. Still, you've got to start somewhere, and that's as good a place as any. That year we did get him going and he won quite a few classes. I never let him go against the clock, I always made him go slow and jump a clear round, then another, then another. He was on his way.

Walking Hickstead

The following year, our Robert caught me filling in the entry forms for Hickstead.

'Ey oop, old feller,' he said (both lads call me 'old feller', I don't know why because I'm not that much of an antique, even now). 'Ey oop, can I go to Hickstead with you?'

I got to thinking about it. Whatever I may have said in my time about Hickstead, or done at Hickstead, or written about it in another part of this book, Dougie Bunn does provide a facility down there. All the kids can have a go, and there's a little ring up in the top corner where they can jump for a pound a round (or it was in those days), and have as many turns as they want. That might be good for Robert, I thought.

'Aye,' I said to him, 'of course you can come.'

So we arrived in the wagon at Hickstead, and I stood in the field and watched my five international horses being unloaded. A million dollars they were worth, and they looked it in their fancy rugs. Last down the ramp was Robert's scraggy old pony which still hadn't recovered from the mauling he'd given it the year before.

The first morning, Robert said: 'Come on, old feller, are you coming over with me?'

He was raring to go. They start in those top rings at nine o'clock, so I had time. I thought: All right, I'll go. The proud father – presenting his son to Hickstead and the world. All in one bloody smack.

Off I went with him. Robert had been going well at shows near home, so we'd see what happened. When we got there, I was left in the entrance to the ring, like any parent, holding the pony.

I started to watch all the kids setting off to walk the course. Kids have got a universal language, it doesn't matter what they speak at home, whether it's French, or English or Spanish, they all somehow get on together. This lot at Hickstead were mostly English but they'd come

66

from all over the place. Within five minutes they were laughing and chatting together and telling jokes. They set off. Now, when you walk the course you're meant to be looking at the jumps. Unfortunately, one of these lads had got out his packet of bubble-gum and handed it round. As they came up to the first fence they were all busy popping away at this bubble-gum.

As I watched, I thought: My God, I'm paying for this! They walked straight past the first fence, told jokes between the second, third and fourth and never saw a single one of them. All of a sudden, they were whacking at buttercups with their sticks, knocking the heads off. That kept them busy past a few more fences, then they finished the round and Robert came over to me. I asked him what he thought of the fences.

'Them fences in there?' he said. 'There's nowt to jump. They're that small, you can hardly see 'em.'

I said: 'You've not been looking for 'em.'

'How d'you mean?' he said.

'Well,' I said, 'you never walked that double.'

'Oh,' he said, 'I never bother walking doubles if they look like that. Old Blackie just jumps them and takes care of them himself.'

I said: 'When you see a double, you step it out and it should be seven yards between the two. If it is, that's about right. When you jump it, you go in at a nice even pace, jump, land, take one stride and jump out. If it's eight yards, you kick in a bit faster and it's easier for the pony. If it's shorter than seven yards, go in a bit slower.'

'That's a good idea!' said Robert.

'Aye,' I said, 'it's not so bad. And what about that ditch up there, under number three?'

He said: 'What ditch?'

'There's a ditch under that third fence up there,' I told him.

'No, there isn't,' he said.

I said: 'There *is*.'

He said: 'Oh, er, ah, oh, don't worry about that. Old Blackie jumps them every day when we're riding on the moor.'

'All right,' I said. We got him warmed up for his round and off he went. He jumped one, he jumped two. They came to three, and old Blackie spied the ditch. He shot Robert straight into it. His wellington boots fell on this side of the bank, his hat fell on the other side, and there in the middle was I, picking up the bits – and Robert. When I'd got all his kit together I shoved it at him.

'Get yourself round that ring,' I said, 'and don't bloody show us up any more.'

Well, he finished his course and came out. 'Robert Smith,' said the announcer – just as I was trying to convince him he'd done well – 'Forty-four and a half faults.'

Next day he asked me: 'Are you coming down, old feller?'

'No,' I said. 'Oh no. Not today.'

On the third day it was coming up to the end of the show. 'Come on, old feller,' he said to me. 'It's the championship today.'

I said: 'How did you go yesterday?'

'Oh,' he said, 'only four faults yesterday.'

All right, I thought, I'll have a look at how he's going on. We got to the ring, and he was all for leaving me at the entrance holding the pony, like on the first day. So I grabbed him quick.

'Come here you,' I said. 'You're going round with me.'

So we set off. 'When you walk a course,' I told him, 'you walk straight through the middle at the start, and then you walk up the middle of all the fences in exactly the route that your pony's going to go on.'

'Yeah,' he nodded.

'And when you get to the end, you sweep round the ends in a nice curve, not in jerks and jiggles but nice and smooth, and then you go down the next line of fences. I've told you about doubles before, but don't forget to measure that out. Then at the end, you go through and finish.'

'Right,' he said. 'Smashing.'

'Have you been having any other problems?' I asked him.

'Aye,' he said, 'I have! He's a little divil.'

'What do you mean?'

'Well, when he's going in a straight line, he's good. But when I get to the end of the ring, and I have to turn, I pull his head round but he just keeps galloping straight on.'

'Pull his head round a bit more,' I said.

'Oh,' he said, 'if I do that – he bites me boot!'

'Don't be stupid,' I said. 'When you're coming down in a straight line, just turn in a bit and bounce him off the rails.'

'Oh,' said Robert, 'that's a good idea!'

Anyway, off he went to put all this wisdom into practice. He started jumping – one, two, three… He got down as far as the end, but then he couldn't get his angle right – and jumped straight out into the cars!

But Not Before the Bell

So that was Robert started at Hickstead. The next place I thought of that was a bit special, was Southport. It's the one place in England where the kids love to go and jump. All the ingredients are right. At an ordinary show you go round and you find there's about twenty to thirty ponies in a class. At Southport, there's a hundred and twenty. So off we went to try it.

It's on the coast, with a big beach, so these kids persuade their mothers and fathers to bring the caravan and the wagon and sit themselves down at Southport for a week. The kids have a great do, and that's why they have a hundred and twenty to a class. Another thing about Southport is that the ground's a little bit dodgy and deep there, so they don't get many clear rounds.

This particular day, our Robert was 117th to go out of 120. There'd only been three clear rounds. I said to him:

'Come on, old lad, you're going to be in clover today. You'll win it.'

Oh, and he looked so young and enthusiastic. He had knicker elastic under his chin and he stared at you with his eyes lit up and his ears stuck out like taxi doors hanging open. I warmed him up outside the ring, and had another look at the pony. It was right on top form.

You can always tell when a pony's jumping out of its skin. It runs down and jumps the fence, then it hangs in the air for five minutes so you can take a picture of it, lands and goes on again. That's when you know they're really at their best.

So I got him all revved up, and into the ring. 'Now come on, old lad,' I told him, 'you can do this. But whatever else you do, don't go before the bell.'

The week before, he'd been in a jump-off at Wetherby. There were four ponies in the jump-off, and he had three of them. The first horse went – the one that wasn't his – and had sixteen faults.

'Well,' I said, 'that's first, second and third for you, Robert. No problem. We're in clover. Get on.'

Off he went on his first pony, but he started before the bell. Eliminated. He went in with the second pony, and missed out the fourth jump. Eliminated. In with the third; missed out the sixth fence. Eliminated.

So that's him eliminated on all three horses. Do you know, when he came out of the main arena into the collecting ring, the crowd actually booed when I pulled him off and battered him!

Anyway, in the ring at Southport, I patted the horse on the backside as it went past and said to Robert: 'Remember. Don't go before the bell.'

Off he went, circling the ring. Up on one side of the crowd, the judge sat in his box. Judges! The one thing in life those people would rather do is eliminate a kid for going before the bell. They don't mind leaving the kids to mill about for five minutes, or what must seem like five minutes, but heaven help them if they go early.

This time, Robert was sensible and waited. At long last the bell went, and there he was, tearing through the start. He jumped the first, and in the crowd I started to shuffle forward. All parents do it. As their son or daughter goes round inside the ring, so they shuffle forward to get a better view. Then they go forward some more. Shuffle forward, shuffle forward. Their ideal viewing position would be underneath each fence!

Then they start the acrobatics. Each time the kid comes to a fence, up goes one foot in sympathy. As the kid gets further into the round, they get more anxious and they lift their foot up higher. At a water jump they do an amazing lift, hover and slide forward through the air till the kid lands. Some parents fall over at water jumps even if the kid stays on.

When Robert came to the double, and jumped it, he had me kicking holes in the air, and when he came to the last, and jumped it, I leapt seven foot straight up. When I came down again, what did he do? Missed the bloody finish, that's what.

A Right Pair

At the same show, Robert and Steven were in the pairs. Well, if it's not bad enough getting one kid on one pony to jump the fences, in pairs events you have to get two kids on two ponies jumping the fences at the same time. As well as the usual faults, if they go one length apart they get a fault for bad dressing.

For six months Robert and Steven had been telling me they were going to win the pairs at Southport. Around the farm they were galloping over walls, hedges and fences, rounding up sheep – stuck together like Siamese twins. I thought: They're not kidding this time. They're going to really do it.

At Southport I was warming up these two ponies who were on their best form. They'd also had it well drilled into their heads that they'd not got to touch a fence. One was twenty-two and one was

twenty-three, so they had a bit of experience between them.

'Right, lads,' I said, 'get into that ring and give it to 'em.'

They went off at the start at a hundred miles an hour. Just as well because they'd be judged on time. They were flying. Clapped together, these little ponies shooting their legs out, they flew round the fences – one, two, three, four…

The fifth fence at the top was set at a bit of an angle. Both ponies arrived at it wrong. So they backed up, then screwed their little legs furiously in the air – and got all eight of them interlocked. Over they went and landed in an almighty heap at the back of the fence.

I ran the hundred yards up that ring faster than Alan Wells could do it. As I got near, I could hear screaming and shouting coming from under the ponies. I thought: There must be a broken leg in there. I got the ponies' legs untied, pulled one off one way and one off the other. When I got down to the kids, they took no notice of me – they were fighting.

'I'm not going with you any more!' 'That's it! I've had it up to bloody here with you!' And hitting each other with their sticks, unmercifully, on the floor. I got them picked up, and I put our youngest on one pony.

'Look, Steven,' I said. 'Go and jump three fences.'

'I'm not jumping…'

'Get down that side!'

Off he went, and I put Robert on the other pony and sent him off to jump three fences on the other side.

As we were leaving the ring, I patted Robert's pony on the backside and said to him: 'It's just one of those things that happens. A chance in a million.'

By this time, Steven was round the other side. Shaking his pony to bits, he was; like me, he's got a bit of a temper, he's a bit sharp. As he came out of the ring, a kid said to him:

'Hee hee hee! You fell off, didn't you?'

Wallop! Steven was off and hitting him faster than the eye could follow. Then they were down in the sand fighting like wild things – blood and snot everywhere. So now I had an extra kid with a bloody nose to look after.

They quietened down quick enough, but the moral of it is this. When a kid's made a mistake, no matter what sport he's in, there's nobody knows better than him what he's done wrong. So parents can best help by doing nothing at first. Just let the lad alone for five minutes, to collect himself.

The Volvo Kid

Robert made the move up to big horses very easily. One night, Steven came into the kitchen. He'd been riding Black Boy in the championship at Hull Show.

'How did you get on today?' I asked him.

'Oh,' he said, 'I won it, I won it real.'

That was the last class of the year for him. I said: 'We're going to have to find you some 14.2 ponies for next year.'

'No,' he said, 'I'm not going to bother with 14.2 ponies.'

'Well, what are you going to do?' I asked him.

'I'm going straight on to big horses.'

I said: 'When are you going to do that?'

He said: 'Tomorrow.'

I said: 'Where the hell am I going to find a big horse for you, straight away like that?'

'Weeell,' he said, 'you'll have summat resting in the field, or one that isn't good enough for you... There must be summat I can take, surely?'

I got thinking. At that stage of my career I had a horse called Volvo, which was a raving bloody lunatic. It was just like a punch-drunk boxer. Every time the bell rang, it didn't jump up and batter some bugger, it jumped up and ran and jumped fences. That's all it needed, the sound of the bell, and it was a maniac. It jumped everything in its sight. Don't get me wrong, the horse was a good 'un. I used to take it to Germany for a fortnight and nobody could get near it – couldn't touch it. It was fast, it went high and wide and did everything. And then it just used to go bananas. My missus knew what it could do, because she'd seen me on it.

'Aye,' I said to Steven. 'I have got a horse for you.'

75

He said: 'What's that?'

I said: 'Volvo. It's in the field.'

He sort of half-looked at me and his mother said: 'Volvo? You're trying to kill my boy!'

I said: 'No, I'm not. He'll look after him. You'll see. There's two classes at that show tomorrow. Hundred pounds Open. Second against the clock. All right.'

There was also a six-bar, which meant you had six fences and they kept going higher and higher. Well, the more you took Volvo into the ring, the barmier it got. After a bit, it went over the top completely.

I said: 'Whatever you do, Steven, forget the six-bar. Don't go in that.'

'All right,' he said.

So I got the saddle and bridle out for him, and then I gave him his orders. 'When you take him to the show, don't point him at anything. Just walk about quietly. If the bell rings, and he sees a bus coming, he'll run and jump it.'

'Aye,' he said, 'all right.'

'What you do,' I went on, 'is go in the collecting ring, and let him jump one or two fences – no more, and one's better than two. Then, when the horse in front of you walks into the ring, the minute that horse has got started, you wander quietly in there too. When the other horse has finished its round, you get yourself over near the start.'

'Whatever for?' said Steven.

'Because,' I said, 'when that bloody bell rings, you want to be in the right position – and going in the right direction!'

'But how do I turn?' he wanted to know.

'Oh, it'll turn all right,' I said.

'Right,' he said. 'And what about the jump-off?'

'Same procedure,' I told him. 'Just you sit there and point him.'

Next night, home he came and sat in the kitchen, scoffing his tea down. He was a man of few words in those days, and I got a real yes-no interview out of him.

'How did you get on today?'

'All right.'

'How did that horse go?'

'Oh, not so bad.'

'Well, how did it go on?'

'I won it.'

'Oh, well done.'

Then he got a bit more chatty. 'Bloody 'ell,' he said. 'When the bell went for the jump-off, he went off that fast I nearly fell off the back of him!

'Turn?' he went on, 'Did he turn? I won it with five seconds to spare. Nobody could get near me.'

'Oh, well done,' I said. 'Have you put it back in the field?'

'Yes,' he said.

'Now, then,' I said to his mother, 'you're better now, aren't you? A hundred quid better off.'

She said: 'How do you mean, a hundred quid better off?'

He said: 'A hundred quid?'

'Well,' I said, 'it was a hundred quid to the winner.'

'Oh,' he said, 'I went in for the six-bar, an' all.'

'You silly little sod!' I said, 'I told you not to go in that. You'll drive that horse proper crackers.'

'I won it,' he said.

He ate on a bit longer, telling us how he'd done this and how he'd done that. All of a sudden he started strumming his fingers. When

he does that, you know there's a crack coming.

'You know,' he said, 'coming home tonight in that wagon, I've been thinking. I was thinking about where you've gone wrong with that horse.'

'Bloody hell,' I said, 'I've been trying for six or seven years to find out where I went wrong with it. So what d'you reckon? What was it?'

He said: 'That horse has been having jockey trouble.'

So that was Robert and Steven launched on the big horses. They've been doing it ever since. Off and on, that's to say. I wouldn't call them idle, but they're the only lads I know who get up in the morning with nowt to do – and go to bed with only half of it done!

ALTAR ROCK – A TRAGEDY

've had upsets with other horses, but nothing as bad as what happened to Altar Rock.

I bought him off a feller called Terry Wharton, at Rufforth. He wasn't expensive, I think I paid about £600 for him. He was a big grey four-year-old, by Sea Serpent. In his first year of showjumping he proved he was a complete natural – the only horse I could ever compare with Farmer's Boy.

It was unheard-of how quickly he came through; by the time I'd had him about four months, he was Grade A – a top competition horse.

He was second in the Suffolk county championship in the first week in June, and he'd won several good open classes besides. This horse was so good, he was a freak.

I was home one day, out walking with the missus and the dog, and we saw a farm on the hilltop. I said to her: 'One day we'll own that.'

Some time later she rang me up when I was at a show. She said: 'That farm is for sale.'

I asked her how much they wanted for it and she said it was £7,500. I said: 'Well, don't let nobody slip in. Go and buy it.'

That night she went and bought it. So I had to start scheming how I was going to get £7,500. As it happened, I was riding O'Malley for Robert Hanson who wanted another top international horse. I rang him up that night and asked him if he was interested in buying Altar Rock.

He said: 'Yes, I'll have him, to pass the vet.'

'He's yours,' I said. 'He's £7,500.'

I thought: That's a good do. I've got my farm bought, and I've still got the horse to ride. I was in clover – a class job.

I came home from the show, feeling as pleased as Punch, and spoke to Mr Hanson again. He said he had a vet at York who would examine the horse.

'OK,' I said, 'there's a show out at Spalding Moor on Saturday. I'll get the horse vetted, then go on to the show and I'll ring you on Saturday night.'

Came Saturday, I took the horse to York and the vet passed him one hundred per cent. I went to the show and the horse won the open class, and we went home again. I rang Mr Hanson and told him the horse had passed the vet and he said fine, he'd be down Tuesday or Wednesday to pay me for him.

On the Monday morning we had the blacksmith in, and all the horses were shod. Next day one of the grooms came scuttling down to the house to find me.

'Come and look at this big grey horse,' she said. 'He's not right.'

I went up there thinking: Gee, here we go. If ever something is wrong in the stable, it's always your best horse.

I got to the stable and this horse, Altar Rock, was in a poor state. He was in a lather all over, and standing leant on the wall, acting like he was punch drunk. This is a queer job, I said to myself, and went in to him. While I was trying to hold him up, he trapped me against the wall and broke my shoulder, but finally we got him laid out on the floor and sent for the vet.

When the vet came, we rolled the horse onto its back, and pulled him out through the door and got him into the paddock so we had plenty of room round him. The vet examined this horse for five or six hours, and came to the conclusion that he must have rolled in his stable and knocked his head on the stone trough in the corner. A completely freak accident; now he was paralyzed down one side.

'What are we going to do for him?' I asked the vet.

'Well,' he said, 'there's a clot pressing on a nerve in his brain. That's why he's paralyzed. To get rid of it, there's some new stuff out that's being used on humans who've been in car crashes. You mix it with a lot of sugar and put it into the bloodstream and it disperses the clot. I think we should give him some of that.'

I thought that sounded alright, so the vet got some of this stuff and pumped it into the horse. Then we started a vigil, sitting up with him day and night. When a horse is ill like this, it has to have people there to turn it over every four or five hours, otherwise it gets congestion of the lungs and quickly dies.

We kept turning him and doing what we could, and he started to improve. On the fifth day, he stood up. He got himself up and just stood there for five minutes, then he got down again. I thought: Great, we're winning. So we kept on with the treatment, and he got up and down again. Then, lo and behold, in about three hours he suddenly took a turn for the worse.

He never recovered, and the vet said afterwards that he'd died of pneumonia. Whether the shock of the accident had something to do with it, we don't know, but we'd got him over the injury which paralyzed him. What finally did for him was pneumonia from being down and unable to move for so long.

Losing that horse was harder than any other loss I've ever had. It was a tragedy. He had so much potential, so much life in front of him, that to lose him in a million-to-one accident knocked me really sideways.

Also, I was now back to square one. I had the farm to pay for, but no money coming in for the horse. I knew one thing: I had to get my jacket off and start working again. I loaded straight up, and went down to a show at Richmond, and won three classes one after the other. I was battling again!

When I think about it, it's strange how you can think you're on top one minute, and be down at the bottom of the heap the next. I'd thought I was in clover, but I hadn't allowed for Mother Nature who has a way of intervening. 'Whoah, you,' she says, 'you're doing too well.' And gives you a thumping – just to make sure you don't forget who's who.

THE NIGHT WE LOST THE LION

Horses and dogs are fine, but I like other animals too, especially if they're a bit unusual. One day I heard of a feller who had a lion for sale, just a young 'un, a female. I thought that would be a good do, so I bought it, put it in the boot of the car and drove it home.

This lion was a good pet, it used to follow me round the place. No trouble at all. Perhaps I got a bit overconfident with it, because what happened next I usually leave to others to tell. I mean, I don't think it's that funny, but the rest of our family have been laughing about it ever since. Our Steven can tell you the story.

Steven: 'After he'd had this lion a few days, he seemed to think it was a dog. One night he had it with him while he was working in the stables. When he'd finished, he opened the door, said: "Come on, lass," whistled for the lion to follow him and walked back to the house.

He came indoors, sat down and forgot about it. Half an hour later, he was muttering: "Bloody 'ell, I wonder where that lion is." So he nipped back outside to look for it. He could see nothing. Nothing at all. He looked all round the stables, in the school, nothing. More time went by, and you could see the panic rising. He ran round everywhere and turned on all the lights in the place. The spotlights were blazing, and from the road we must have looked like an ocean liner. He ran all the way round the back of the buildings. Still nothing.

He pulled me out to his car, a brand-new Merc. "Get in," he said.

I didn't fancy it much, because I was going out that night. I had the smart gear on, the beboppy shoes and all that stuff. Anyway, I got in the car and he shot off round the corner to the gate.

It was knee deep in mud when I got out and opened the gate. Then the car got stuck and I had to push it. The old feller was in a fine old mood by then. Sweating. The car was good and stuck, so he jumped out and started running down our road. I don't know if he knew where he was going but just then my mother arrived in her car and turned in towards the house. When she saw the old feller running at her in the headlights, she stopped.

"What's happening?" she asked him. "Why are all those lights on up there?"

That was as far as she got, because he opened the door, pulled her out on the road, jumped in and drove off across the field, looking for this lion. But no matter which way he turned, he couldn't find it. It was nowhere. Then he started thinking about the moors, perhaps it was up there. He had no chance of taking a car onto the moors so he came racing back to the house.

By then me and Robert and our mother were stood around busting ourselves laughing. The old feller wasn't best pleased about that, then I heard him shouting at me about my bike.

"Get me that bike going," he said, meaning my little 50 cc trail bike.

I said: "What for?"

He said: "Cos I'm going over the moors and I'm going to find that lion."

We got the bike out for him and he was in the saddle in a flash and kicking at the starter.

"Listen," I said to him, "you've got to be careful with that, 'cos the throttle's stuck full open and won't shut off."

He took no notice, just kicked it half to death until it fired – and when it did that bike stood up on its back wheel and went like an arrow down the back lane. It went a full one hunded yards on one wheel and turned over in the ditch at the top.

He'd never been on a bike in his life, and it showed. Me and Robert were left shouting "Whoah!" after him all the way to the ditch, and laughing our heads off. Then he came storming back down the lane and sent us back in the house.

"Right, you," he was shouting, "you're useless. You can get in that house and stay there!"

We went into the kitchen and sat on the edge of the table with our mother, looking out of the window. Every so often we had a glimpse of him running past in the field, right to left then he disappeared out of view, then back he came the other way, left to right and disappeared. We were screaming with laughter already, but each new time we saw him, the hysterics got worse till it was painful to go on laughing.

It wasn't just him that was funny. It was a catastrophe out there – cars everywhere and things smashed up all over the place, a lion gone missing, it was so ridiculously out of control that we were helpless from laughing at it.

All of a sudden the old feller came up to the window and started banging on it. Now he was pointing at my mother. We opened the window so we could hear him. He was deadly serious.

"If you think you're laughing at me," he said to our mother, "you can go to bed."

Mother had to leave the kitchen and go upstairs. So that was her sent off. Me and Robert were still laughing about that – when all of a sudden the lion appeared through the door, quiet as anything, and looked at us.

It had been round the corner the whole time in the shed – the one place he hadn't looked. We found out later that this was typical of lions – if they're left alone, they don't go away from buildings. If only someone had known that before. But it wouldn't have been half so funny.'

Thanks very much, Steven. I'll see you later.